HOW I LEARNED TO BE WHITE

ALSO BY TRICIA KNOLL

Broadfork Farm (2017)
Ocean's Laughter (2015)
Urban Wild (2014)

HOW I LEARNED TO BE WHITE

Poems by

Tricia Knoll

Antrim House
Simsbury, Connecticut

Copyright © 2018 by Patricia A. Knoll

Except for short selections reprinted for purposes of
book review, all reproduction rights are reserved.
Requests for permission to replicate should
be addressed to the publisher.

Library of Congress Control Number: 2018933859

ISBN: 978-1-943826-47-6

First Edition, 2018

Printed & bound by Ingram Content Group, LLC

Book design by Rennie McQuilkin

Front cover photograph by Carolyn Martin

Author photograph by Robert R. Sanders

Antrim House
860.217.0023
AntrimHouse@comcast.net
www.AntrimHouseBooks.com
21 Goodrich Road, Simsbury, CT 06070

This book is dedicated to Mabel Purifoy, who took me by the hand, knowing far more about me than I knew about her.

And to Annie Dunn, my great-grandmother, whose name I bear as a middle name and who handed down the letters her brothers and fiancé wrote from Union army battle lines in six states over long, war-weary years.

To my German ancestors.

To teachers in racial justice programs.

To my community, friends, and family – especially my husband – for his patience with my questions and concerns about white privilege.

ACKNOWLEDGMENTS

Grateful acknowledgment to the editors of the following publications in which poems in this volume first appeared, at times in earlier versions:

JOURNALS

Gyroscope Review: "Portland's Waterfront History"

Hamilton Stone Review: "White Girls"

HEArt (Human Equity Through Art) Journal: "My Mother, the Police, and Me"

So It Goes (a publication of the Kurt Vonnegut Memorial Library): "William Lewis' Letters to Miss Annie"

Social Justice Poetry: "The Night I Didn't Stand Up"

New Verse News: "My Six-Month DAR Membership," "Let's Hear It for the Horses"

Verse-Virtual: "Letters from Union Soldiers"

Visual Verse: "Compassion"

ANTHOLOGIES

Sparrow's Trill – Writers Respond to the Charleston Shooting (Minerva Rising Literary Journal): "Body Language"

To Wake, To Rise: Meditations on Justice and Resilience (Skinner House Books): "Connecting"

What Rough Beast (Indolent Books): "Portland's ICE Center As the Crow Flies"

TABLE OF CONTENTS

Connecting / 3
Mabel / 4
Deerfield, Illinois, 1959 / 6
The Black and White Photo of My Mother on the Front
    Porch in 1960 / 8
Marching As To War / 9
Lynn's Birthday Party, May 1955 / 10
Yom Kippur - the Longest Day of Seventh Grade / 12
The Retired Prison Warden / 13
The Blue Samsonite Suitcase / 14
Wild Turkeys / 15
The Teenager Talks About Her Grandmother / 16
Letters from Union Soldiers / 18
William Lewis' Letters to Miss Annie / 19
My Mother, the Police, and Me / 20
Shooter Doings / 22
From the Dance Floor / 23
Advanced Placement American History / 24
We Were So Quiet in Our House / 25
In Defense / 26
But / 27
Tall Man Sam / 28
DNA / 29
The Portrait of the Rulachs, Circa 1850 / 30
Hillhouse High School, New Haven, Connecticut, 1970-72 / 31
Carpooling with Helen, 1973 / 33
My Adopted Wedding Ring / 34
My Six-Month DAR Membership / 35
Out from the Wash / 37
Mardi Gras Beads / 38
Portland's Waterfront History / 39
The Night I Didn't Stand Up / 40

The White Peacock / 41
White Girls / 42
Body Language / 43
Ebony and Ivory / 44
Nomenclature / 46
Let's Hear It for the Horses / 47
Out of My Dream of a Man in a White Sheet
  Carrying a Sign: THIS IS WRATH / 48
Portland's ICE Center As the Crow Flies / 49
Simple Signs & Messages / 51
The Star Guard / 52
Who Am I to Say? / 53
Three Blind Women March on Washington / 54
Why My Pussy Hat Is Purple with a Stretched
  Thread of Silver Silk / 55
Compassion / 56

Notes / 58
About the Author / 59
About the Book / 60

white is not a given
point extended line

blank for signing

– Martha Collins

My own luck was being born white and middle-class
into a house full of books...

– Adrienne Rich

What kind of people were we, Jean Louise? What kind
of people are we?

– Dr. Finch to Jean Louise in Harper Lee's* Go Set a Watchman*

This is what you shall do: love the earth and sun, and animals, despise riches, give alms to every one that asks, stand up for the stupid and crazy, devote your income and labor to others, hate tyrants . . . go freely with the powerful uneducated persons, and with the young, and mothers, of families . . . re-examine all you have been told at school or church, or in any books, and dismiss whatever insults your own soul . . . .

– Walt Whitman

HOW I LEARNED TO BE WHITE

Connecting

I'm white space
between black dots.
I grew up catching tigers
by the toe. School books
came with unbroken backs.

No one ever called my people X.
Families on TV looked like mine.
I believed money could get me
where I wanted to go.

I own the land I live on.
I was never a melting anything –
fondue, chocolate, molten pot,
hot lava lamp, or zombie brain.

A bubble surrounds me,
shimmer-soap surprise
I thought would never pop
until it did.

Mabel

Some weekends she took care of us.
Or cleaned. When Mabel fried chicken,
my mother complained the stove got
so greasy she had to scrub it all over again.

For Mabel's break I got a cup of Postum
heavy with sugar and whole milk.
We held the handles with two fingers
like fine ladies. Her last name, she said,
was French. For faithful and true.

The first black person I knew,
her gentle "bazoom"
as she called it, so big and soft.
How Mabel held me.

One steamy July, I asked her why
her skin was dark and mine was light.
She led me to my mother's garden.
First to the lilacs my father babied.

Then we touched rose petals,
smelled yucky marigolds.
She showed me faces on Grandmother's pansies
and how snapdragons pinch fingers.

She said we were flowers,
all the garden colors together
made it the best it could be.
She held my hand.

At four-thirty she walked to the train
back to the south side of Chicago

carrying her cloth shopping bag.
I watched her amble down the block.

Swollen feet, beige hose bagging,
her low-heeled shoes
so worn down
her ankles fell in.

I never knew exactly where she went.
I missed her right away.
Why didn't she get new shoes?

Deerfield, Illinois, 1959

In November of 1959 a sorry joke began to make the rounds in Chicago, particularly in the northern suburbs. It went something like this: What is the definition of a three-time loser? A man who bought an Edsel, put in a crop of cranberries, and purchased a house in Deerfield.

– Harry and David Rosen, *But Not Next Door*

I was 12. Ice tea with sugar. Pogo sticks. To the basement
to play Monopoly during tornadoes. A red bike.
A gold dog. Whitefish dinner at noon on Sundays.
Homegrown tomatoes splitting in early fall.
Stinking dead alewives on Ravinia Beach
in Highland Park, our town.

One afternoon my mother helloed
to Mrs. Pearson over the trash cans, marigolds
and flagstones that separated our back doors.
They whispered. I perked up. Whispers?

> *Will Martin Luther King come?*
> *Will there be trouble?*

What I wasn't supposed to hear.

*

It took me more than fifty years to find out why. Deerfield Township halted integration with a stop-work order on a housing development named Floral Park. A development of 51 homes on 22 acres, 10 or 12 to sell to families of color for about $30,000 a home. A Little-Rock-of-Illinois metaphor became Chicago's front-page news. Then national.

The developers? Well, the corporation's board and advisors included Jacob Javits, Oscar Hammerstein, Rev. Martin Luther

King Jr., Bishop Pike, Roy Wilkins, and Eleanor Roosevelt. The local Presbyterian, Unitarian, Lutheran, Episcopal, and Bethlehem United Brethren clergy wrote a unified statement of support. The Catholics urged parishioners to act in the tradition of Christianity.

Public meetings ensued in school gyms. TV cameras showed up. Radio. Rantings I never heard. A handful blamed Communists. Human rights groups lobbied for integration.

In November people charged the developers with sneakiness. Then volunteers polled residents: 8 to 1 – homeowners did not approve of an integrated housing project.

In December the cry, More parks! although two ballot measures for parks had recently failed. Voters passed a bond referendum four days before Christmas to condemn Floral Park, zone it for parks. This scrub of milkweed, dandelions and quack-grass.

Early court decisions upheld Deerfield's authority to condemn land.

*

My class of 1965 was the first to graduate from the new Deerfield High, a top-percentage school that earned a reputation for sending students to top-percentage universities. No one in my class was black.

The Black and White Photo of My Mother on the Front Porch in 1960

The porch is not generous, no chairs or swings,
a white picket fence around a concrete slab.
You stand ready for church. Tortoise-shell buttons

on a cashmere coat that hangs
below your knees. After war years, you love nylons,
you like Ike. Your family thinks you're pretty.

Your heels are not your highest, not for church, but high enough
to show off good legs. Your tiny hat is not one I would pick –
Jackie Kennedy was making an impact with pillboxes.

You know the camera is on you. Your white-gloved hand
tips on the point of a picket. Your right heel plants
against the arch of your left foot. A tilt to your head

as if maybe last night you and my father made love
and you suspect he is thinking of that and not yet of church
where he teaches a Sunday school class of teenagers.

We wait, my brothers and I, know the neighbors
see our little tableau, how different we are.
They do not go to church on Sunday,

they go to temple. Their kids learn Hebrew.
Me, a gawky girl in black patent-leather shoes,
I see how your feet pose, wish you would

pet our dog more, not wear white gloves. I knew
until the day you died, I would not grow up
to be the woman you wanted me to be.

Marching As To War

Chains of church mornings,
I stared out windows over the ravine,
singing *Onward Christian Soldiers*.

As to what war I never knew.
Who was our enemy? The body?
We didn't believe in doctors.

I had that ear infection.
My parents paid an old lady
smelling of bottled lilacs

to pray for me. Warts fell off
my soles. My Sunday school teacher
who explained my healing

shook with Parkinson's.
I did learn fractions at her table,
figuring percentages of time

left each Sunday to annoy her.
Practice at manipulating math
served me later, pinpointed

where I was in a marathon run,
what part of my life was spent
with each man who took me on.

I grew up to learn how rarely
armies move gracefully
into going on before.

Lynn's Birthday Party, May 1955

All the girls in the neighborhood were invited. My Girl Scout troop that snacked on lox, bagels and cream cheese. The girls who walked the mile-and-a-half to third grade. That wide net included me.

She made her wishes, blew out candles. Her father reached to put chocolate cake with vanilla ice cream in front of me. I waited until everyone was served. Ice cream melted in clammy before-a-rainstorm heat.

I asked him, "Why do you have numbers on your arm?"

That snuffed the girl-talk. The others looked at plates edged in pink roses.

He pulled back his arm. His fingers brushed my shoulder. "When you get home, ask your mother."

I did not ask. Over the years I saw how the German-American on my father's side played out in this town of others with cut-off roots in Eastern Europe. My grandfather left Germany in the 1880s to avoid the Prussian draft. Many of our neighbors left Germany in fear of Nazis and lost those left behind. I never heard my second-generation father speak a word of German. In December once he sang "Tannenbaum" in the shower.

My father buried stinky German cheese in glass Mason jars in snow because my mother wouldn't allow it in the refrigerator. His factory in North Chicago made printers' hand tools. He ate hasenpfeffer, Weiner Schnitzel and sauerbraten for lunch at the Schwaben Stube on North Lincoln Avenue most weekdays. At the "round table" reserved for bent-over men of German ancestry who owned factories. I liked the Stube's murals of a story about a German miser and his goat. Stollen and strudels he brought home from Dinkels on Saturday mornings.

Few houses near us hung out Christmas lights. Brilliant reds and greens and blues under the falling snow illuminated who lived at our house.

Yom Kippur – the Longest Day of Seventh Grade

My father was president of the school board.
Jewish holiday or not, I was going to school.
He insisted there were other Christian children
in the three seventh-grade classes.

I was the only seventh grader who showed up.

I clapped erasers, set loose drifts of yellow chalk.
Two math worksheets, dittoed. Then six hours
in the fourth seat by a window levered open
to let in the dust of oak leaves drying in September wind.
Me and empty chairs. I read about wind-swept moors,
chipped at the blue-ink rut of some boy's desk graffiti.
A janitor pushed a wide mop in parallel lines.
I counted. How often my foot jerked.
How the clock lurched when the big hand
hit six. Breaths per minute.

Three teachers kibitzed up front,
hushed so gossip couldn't go home with me.
One teacher stank of cigarettes.
Without the clang of lockers,
a ghost town of shrill bells.

The Retired Prison Warden

I barely knew Grandpa Carl Lewis.
I remember that one black-and-white photo
of him beside his thin-armed wife.
In his Florida citrus grove
he kept a Doberman for show
to scare black migrants
who arrived each season
to pick his navel oranges,
luscious oranges he handed us
with broken peppermint sticks,
straws to suck out juice.

The Blue Samsonite Suitcase

I am not sure how many trips it made with me with its blue satin curtain between half sides, billowy blue pockets. When laid out flat, one side was for my underwear and t-shirts and the other for jeans and jackets. Who used it before me, I don't know.

Now it holds photos my mother saved. Only one of my grandmother who looks nervous beside her husband. Carl Lewis, father of my mother, a do-it-my-way, no backtalk, law and order man. He thought it fine to raise his two daughters in Occoquan, Virginia's House of Correction. He was the warden.

That suitcase doesn't have a single picture of the prison – just lace hankies some women inmates tatted for my grandmother that still smell of cologne. I took that lace for show-and-tell in third grade. Told about my mother born in the prison, named Virginia for the state. Told how Grandfather chose the trustee to watch over my mother and her sister – a murderer that he believed took the prison sentence for a sister who did the poisoning. Eventually Grandmother insisted they had to move to another prison in Connecticut. So the girls would grow up outside prison walls.

Carl bought the Dobermans for the orchard and gave my brothers rifles to shoot copperheads. Later he called out the convicts to beat up unionists wanting to organize the garment factory he supervised. My mother said he was strict. She learned how to sneak.

My grandmother is rail thin in her last picture. My father holds her elbow and guides her to our living room.

Just one photo of grandfather and his potbelly. Tucked in blue linings.

Wild Turkeys

Many years after my first husband took to saying how much he liked drinking Wild Turkey, I saw my first wild turkey. My daughter pointed to a small flock wandering around Columbia's Lamont-Doherty Earth Observatory outside New York City. A year later on a broiling August day, on a dirt road outside Sisters, Oregon, one scraggly turkey ran up a gravel road. What was hardest for me to understand was my mother's story about her mother – the grandmother I knew weighed maybe 90 pounds. With transparent skin and dime-size moles on her wattled neck. When I was twelve, she clutched the sides of her bedroom door frame, begging me to grab her and help her to her chair, crying she'd be stronger after her next transfusion. My mother said Grandmother took a rifle into the Kentucky bush and shot Thanksgiving dinner.

> hen scratches
> a shallow nest in leaves
> the outline of my hand

The Teenager Talks About Her Grandmother

When she had nowhere else to go,
my mother brought her to live with us.
Grandmother thought of herself as Kentucky gentile
if never rich. She pinched my fingertips to thin them
so someone would marry me, she said. These hands
my father said would make a fine machinist.

Her stomach was surgically disconnected
from her esophagus. Her room smelled
of desiccated beef liver powder, cod liver oil
and protein meals in the formula she squished
through a long red tube into her gut,
a tube coiled like a snake in a Mason jar.
Her "eating" made swirl-gurgles,
aspirating noises.

My mother did grandmother's laundry,
trimmed her thick yellow toenails.
When my parents were away,
I lift-hauled her, her bones like wands,
to her lounge chair, to the bathroom.
She promised to haunt me after she died.

When my mother moved her into Assisted Living,
floral overtones of ammonia compounded her smell.
I overheard my mother tell my father
that grandmother accused the night nurse,
the only black nurse, of trying to poison her.
The administrator called three times to discuss
"how to handle Mrs. Lewis's claims."
No one believed her. Wrongness
seldom mentioned where I could hear.
A shame my mother endured.

My family never talked
about unpleasant things
like the vomit-gurgle
in Grandmother's bathroom.

After Grandmother choked to death,
no one spoke of a funeral or said where her body went.
I thought it was because we were glad she was gone.

Letters from Union Soldiers

You can't put the past behind you. It's buried in you;
it's turned your flesh into its own cupboard. — Claudia Rankine

Their sixty letters of rusted-iron ink are safe in my
   black-and-gold hatbox
on a high shelf — accounts of mud-sucked marching boots minimize
   their wounds.
I wish they had hated slavery, held bellies on fire to fight to emancipate.
They said they fought to keep a union whole, to halt a dividing house.

On my closet shelf, accounts of mud-sucked marching boots
   minimize suffering
standing picket, aching to hear from home, recounting how many died.
They fought to keep a union whole, to halt a dividing house,
marching with Sherman to the sea. New boots somewhat tight.

They stand sentry. Complain about the cold. Recording how many died,
the Dunns made do. Lewis recounts the goals of engagement
marching with Sherman to the sea. Worn-out boots not quite right,
furloughs postponed, rebel camps less than a mile by, hours in
   six-foot trenches.

The Dunns made do. William Lewis ducked shells, shared
his disdain for the drafted, secessionists and Copperheads, no
   mention of slavery
midst furloughs denied, rebels' dawn musket fire, hours stacked up
   as sentries.
These are my men. Their helix genes twirl down to me.

Disdain for the drafted, secessionists and Copperheads, few mentions
   of blacks.
I wish they had hated slavery, held bellies on fire to fight for freedom.
These men of mine. Intertwining helixes of genes twirl down to me
in handwritten scrawls of blood-rust ink, buried in a bandbox.

William Lewis' Letters to Miss Annie

My great-grandfather William Lewis, a carpenter, mustered into the 13th regiment of the Indiana Infantry in 1862 in a regiment attached to the Army of the Ohio. He was twenty-three, 6'1" with hazel eyes and dark hair according to enlistment documents. He wrote letters like these to Annie Dunn throughout his service, came home to marry her and father my grandfather, Carl Lewis.

Near Deep Bottom, Virginia, August 18, 1864

We left Petersburg after Burnside's defeat. We are now trying to reach Richmond. The greater part of our Division has been wiped out. Breathing nothing but smoke of burning powder and having nothing to eat but solid shot for two or three months might demoralize anyone. I am tired of war.

Richmond, Virginia, November 30, 1864

It is time for me to arouse from my mute unconsciousness. The scenery with which I am surrounded is grand enough to inspire the most phlegmatic with enthusiasm. The gleam of burnished arms. Innumerable banners flutter for miles along our earthworks. The shrill blast of bugles and the merry roll of drums along with brass bands and cheers, jokes, peals of laughter of our battle-scarred veterans. Enough about this lovely scatteration of human habitations. Some 5,000 of us Yanks were taken to New York a few days before the election to suppress the riot which owing to our presence and that of our noble Commander (Beast Butler) did not occur. The election passed off very quiet. Uncle Abe was elected and we returned to our old camp four and a half miles from the rebel capitol.

Virginia, December 10, 1864

I will not promise to write anything interesting. What little brains I used to have are battered out and lost.

My Mother, the Police, and Me

Chicago, Illinois, 1955

I'm eight. My mother drives down West Addison
to a faith-healing dentist, Dr. Otnes,
and takes a hard left turn when we pass his office.
A Chicago squad car flashes her.
She pulls over, sticky with summer. The officer
pulls out his ticket book. I stare at the glove box.

She weeps. He exhales, lips loud.
"My husband is on our school board.
We're going to her dentist. I got turned around.
I'm a church lady." He gives her a warning.
This is the first time I see her cry.

New Haven, Connecticut, 1970

I'm twenty-three. May. Orange Street, blocks
from the Green. Riot police spray tear gas
outside the trial of the New Haven Nine
and Bobby Seale. Gas billows fog. I jog home
and shut my windows. The night is long with yelling
and young people running. The President of Yale
says he doubts black revolutionaries
can get a fair trial anywhere in America.
Two thousand miles away,
my mother knows nothing, believes I'm safe.
Studying.

Rural Clatsop County, Oregon 1989

I'm forty-two. I drive. My mother is passenger.
My daughter snuggles in her car seat
as sunbeams poke through Douglas firs.

A squad car flashes me
for out-of-date license tags. I spout,
"You pulled me over for tags?
I'm from Portland. Where police worry about real crime.
This is all you do, pull people over for license tags?"
My mother slaps my wrist resting on the gearshift.
She's hushing me, "No. No, don't, no," with a tremor.
I take the ticket. We're 80 miles from home.

She starts in about garment union men
with hordes of bed bugs in glass bottles.
She worked in the office where Grandfather
managed a garment factory that employed
mostly ex-cons he knew from the days
when garment factories were inside prison walls.
The union men meant to smash the bottles
inside the factory. My grandfather
blew a whistle. His ex-cons came out swinging
baseball bats. Her tale went on to
Eliot Ness and gunfire. I take her comments
as lessons about men,
not law enforcement.

North Charleston, Carolina, April 4, 2015

I am sixty-seven. My mother is dead.
Today police pull over Walter Scott,
a black forklift operator,
for expired license plate tags.
He winds up shot. Shot dead.
My mother knew more
than I thought she did.
She, the warden's daughter.

Shooter Doings

That black hat box, the letters —
from the dates and locales
I know what my men were doing
more than one hundred and fifty years ago.
Mud, snow, worn-out boots, bare feet,
the zing of shells and death counts.

Annie wrote from back-home
that their good-old dog had distemper.
She shot that mad dog.

Shooters think they know
exactly what they are doing.
That's how police get away
with murder.

From the Dance Floor

She and I swapped stories from the 1960s – like handing over eggplant casserole recipes we might never bake. Her story was she was young and lithe at a rock concert with a frat-boy. The band was black, bass-rhythm heavy throb. The guitar man laid down his instrument and waggled his finger at her blondness. She reached for him; he hoisted her onto the stage. And they danced. Shook it up. Wriggled, hipped and bumped.

At a break, sweaty, she hopped down. And saw lightning in her date's fist. "You're going to hit me? You are going to hit ME?"

For dancing with the musician. "You hit me and I'll call the police and your life will never be the same."

Her storytelling moved on to aging back pain. I was stuck on the dance floor. She grew up to be an attorney assisting battered women. I was a girl who would have danced for sure that night but would never have been waggled at to step up. I bet I never would have been with a man who might hit me. Maybe it was luck.

Advanced Placement American History

These high school history lessons were never Illini stories
of Thunder Beings and Grandmother Earth.
No accounts of Indian Removal. Once an arrowhead.

We cracked open brand-new books to smell clean gutters
and read inaugural addresses, each President in turn:

Manifest Destiny, a story
like Man's dominion.
Words we never heard
in the promises of Presidents –
redlining Deerfield,
exclusion acts, Jim Crow,
privilege we lived
every safe day.

No one ever asked me to open a door
into the garment factory, feel barbs on cotton,
see the jail cell, hear the lynch mobs,
witness forced marches to reservations
or internment camps. Those did not happen
in the class where I studied.

Susan B. Anthony showed up as footnote.
I might have adopted Ida B. Wells as my role model.
Or Mary Eliza Church Terrell. Mamie Till-Mobley.
I'm poorer for learning them late.

We Were So Quiet in Our House

Lamb chops broiled on the grill popped fat whisked out a hood fan. I never heard my grandfather's story about his father's death, how his father died one year after he was born. Why my great-grandfather's son was named Wade when my great-grandfather nearly died in a Mississippi River flood coming home from the Civil War. Someone knew. How the other son Carl became a prison warden. I spent my childhood watching chipmunks run outside on the windowsill, inciting our golden retriever. I had to consider the ineffectiveness against chipmunks of the gas bombs and poison peanuts my father put in their way.

> the mouse at night
> knows the walls
> raceways

In Defense

Isn't this what we do? Balance faults with graces? My father kept the peace between Poles in his factory's shipping room and German machinists. He was an equal-opportunity talker – chatted with anyone and everyone, everywhere. On most Saturday mornings I sat in a Chinese laundry tracing designs in window sweat from the steam pressings. He took his shirts in for light starch, folded. I don't remember a word they said, just how long he talked to the owners, husband and wife. Next we were off to the Jewish jeweler where he kibitzed about school funding while I roamed past glass cases of gold, platinum and pearls, bracelets my father never bought. My dad had been dead for forty years when I learned that as president of the school board, he convinced our wealthier neighbors (and probably the jeweler) to contribute to the down payment on a house for the first black teacher hired in the district.

My mother could nail me in place with one eyebrow lift. But then, she agreed to be the liaison to local high schools for the North Shore Chapter of the Daughters of the American Revolution. She was the youngest of the elderly white women, qualified because she was capable to still drive a car from suburb to suburb to give a DAR award to a graduating senior girl that the school's faculty chose for outstanding scholarship and citizenship. One high school chose a Cherokee woman. The DAR chapter refused to give their award to her. My mother threatened to resign from the DAR on the front-page of the *Chicago Tribune*. The student received her award.

How easy to feel good enough.

But

Try phrases where you don't justify the action you are taking.
      – linguistic advice on the use of the word "but"

Last night a woman began her story "My mother isn't racist, but . . ."

I feared *but* would lead to no good end.

Her mother's embrace of southern traditions learned in Mississippi was more than making biscuits with riced potatoes and buttermilk. Hierarchy, status, privilege, separation and indifference mixed in. I spoke up with an untrained heat on how buts have killed too many people. Her response – "I will defend my mother." Oops. I just did the same.

Roots. I dwell on mine. I ask too much of fifer Jabez Cleveland to have made music in the American Revolution for the oneness of humankind. Then the Dunn boys, foot soldiers in the war on slavery, who spent days standing sentry in deep mud for the good of the Union. I'm the granddaughter of an assistant warden who served in a Virginia prison a year before the suffragettes who chained themselves to Woodrow Wilson's White House fence were locked up there. He left for a promotion. I belong to the NAACP.

But.

Tall Man Sam

Before Christmas 2014, 12-year-old Santana Janis hung herself from a tree in the cold on the Pine Ridge Reservation, one of many in an epidemic of teen suicides there in past years. Elders blame a spirit known as Slender Man, also known as Walking Sam or the Tall Man.

He came to me as Walking Sam. I was seventeen.
I wore a black cowl shirt for thirty weeks
to show I heard his whispers, soft and obscene.
Knife-blades of menace in promises he asks kids to keep.
I dipped my body inside his shadow, planned
to gas myself in a narrow garage. One person cared.
I struggled not to give myself to his killing class.
Through chance. And fear. I was spared.
On the Pine Ridge Rez they call him Tall Man,
faceless, sidling up to teens, dressed in black,
whispering how to give up space. Follow his plan,
bind your neck, echo-breath of sad-sack sickness.
I didn't go to school at Wounded Knee.
And no one called me a filthy Indian.

*

Once he finds an open ear, Walking Sam will return.
Maybe not next month, maybe seasons down the road.
He'll sidle in, cradle an elbow in his palm, list concerns
about loss and woe and worth, a tap on ancient source code.
With age I've grown to see him full, not so slant or cornered
in my eye. His full-on specter faces my elder spirit,
my look ahead, a steady gait, one foot forward
between pills for lowness, talk-help to lay out my limit.
This is what aging sadness filters down to know.
I see no end to Sam's good wooing, yet something internal
insists on interdiction, to up-end him to the low below
of mourning-think, to basements of the deep and personal.
Let him dissolve as today's faint shadow. I am unwilling subject,
strong of body, full of privileged old codes, unable to forget.

DNA

My spit in a tube told me exactly what I knew –
half Anglo-Saxon from the British Isles,

half from eastern Germany.
I had held giddy, romantic hopes

of an indigenous person slipping in,
a one-with-earth breath in my breast,

fantasy of a lover my ancestors kept secret.
First people displaced by the likes of mine.

WASP. What I knew to be true
that afternoon I learned I wasn't a Jew.

The Portrait of the Rulachs, Circa 1850

What do we do with our ancestors? —*Theodore Roethke*

The artist tried to get their faces right —
his high forehead above a square jaw
and sparse black beard,
a stiff woman with a dumpling face,
short-waisted to fit behind her husband,
with one ringless fist
below a lacy scab-red sleeve
resting on his shoulder.
Like a limp starfish caught
in a withdrawing tide.

My brothers don't think
even the wave-scalloped gold frame
makes this ancestral painting worth saving.
Three husbands disliked these Rulachs.
A divorce appraiser declared the portrait
of only sentimental value.

Visitors say the couple is spooky,
expressionless and possibly mean.
So tired they've given up.

How contrary of me to admire
these dour Germans.
I wear her parted-down-the-middle
slicked-back brown hair, share puffiness
below the eyes, and her stubby fingers.
I'd wear an earring like hers.
A tiny silver bell.

Hillhouse High School, New Haven, Connecticut, 1970–72

I am the only colored student in my class.
– Langston Hughes, *Theme for English B*

Student Teaching, 1970

A Yalie come a few hours
each day to this school to practice teach.
This school where one out of four
students never graduated.
Where I seldom got a movie projector
because other schools took better care of them.
Four years older than my students.
I thought I was cool. Real cool.
Twenty-five black students, one white.

My First Full-Time Teaching Assignment, 1970–1971

The year started pacing the sidewalk on strike.
A week later the assistant principal welcomed me
to the faculty, mostly white.
He handed me one key and two rules –
always keep my classroom door locked and never
let students throw books out the window.

Thirty big-print anthologies titled *Prejudice* were to last
six weeks with my ninth-grade Honors English,
these black kids and their brand-new out-of-the box
    white teacher.
I memorized Langston Hughes' *Mother to Son*.
We read Shirley Jackson's *The Lottery*.
No one threw stones.

Apple Cider Gone Hard, 1971

For breakfast I drank local fall apple cider
gone a bit hard. Walking to school I was tipsy
and late. I stuck out my thumb.
A beat-up low-riding black four-door
stopped at the curb. Black male driver.
His wife, I guessed, holding a baby.
Two slouching men in the back
and a teenage boy looking at his lap.
The woman in front slid over.
I asked if they could let me off a block
from school. No one said a word.
I asked the woman if she had apple juice
in her baby's bottle. *No*, the woman said. *Beer.*

Senior Honors English, 1972

We completed *Hamlet* in May
and decided to finish out the year
making a Super 8 movie spoof
with Sly & The Family Stone
as background music.
Willis was the obvious lead.
Tall, the basketball star.
Everyone graduates.
When I Google Willis' name,
the only man the right age
is serving time.

Carpooling with Helen, 1973

We both taught English at a Portland high school in a service boundary that circled two Bible colleges, a golf course, the airport, and a bowling alley. Helen was the school's old guard – white beehive bun, baby-blue polyester pants, a skittish Lady Macbeth. She used seniority to transfer to our school to get out of the inner-city, not that Portland has much, the whitest city in the U.S.

I was newish. Wore mini-skirts. I got into trouble opposing the football team's pre-game prayers and unequal salaries for women coaches.

We shared rides because of an oil embargo, soaring gas prices and long pump lines. We didn't chat much in the morning. I needed more coffee. She couldn't wait to retire. One day she brought up the school district's decision to bus kids to foster desegregation. I stopped for a red light at a five-way intersection. Our school, James Madison High School, was named for a slave-owning President who never freed his slaves and proposed counting each one as 3/5 of a person.

She snapped open the handles of her white purse, withdrew a hanky and wiped her nose. "We'll have to lock up our purses and coats in our classroom closets when the black kids come."

I squinted into December drizzle. Shirley Chisholm said not to stand on sidelines, but my mother hated girls who got uppity.

What could I say to penetrate Helen's girdle of certainties? I flicked the wipers from intermittent to intense. Politeness. Good lord, I wanted to be elsewhere, not mute, staring through amped-up, worn-out wiper blades.

My Adopted Wedding Ring

I'm not certain whose finger it was made for.
I wear it out of convenience. Diamonds
neither my husband nor I paid for,

jewels that crossed the ocean in hems,
immigrants escaping a Prussian draft,
these few saved through the Depression.

I found the ring in my mother's red box
after she died. From my father's mother
on the German side.

Through his loupe a jeweler analyzed
crown and table, glints and facets –
mine-cut, late 1880's.

South Africa's
diamond mines'
stifling heat of exploitation,

a sparkle provenance
I'm wedded to.

My Six-Month DAR Membership

Joining

Jabez Cleveland, a fifer
in the Connecticut 8th regiment
dead, age thirty-eight at Bunker Hill.
He played a simple six-hole flute
of infantry battle calls,
wake-ups, marching tunes
over greens, through woods,
in-the-reeds shepherds' songs
legacy of wind in thigh bone.

His thick blood
trills in my veins.

My grandmother, the warden's widow,
wanted the genealogy grid on her side filled
back to Braintree's Webb House,
that public house seat of battle plans.

My mother did the hard work
chasing down county seats,
resolved records about the traveling peddler
from Kokomo, the bigamist.

Resigning

I thought studying
generals and bravery,
powder horns and compasses,
might help me hear

the stepping fife and drum
that got me here.

Then those bowed gray heads,
women's breasts festooned
with gold pins.
Praying to God
to bless America.

My Jabez plays
to a net-snarled humpback,
to a mother's screams in Gaza,
AIDS orphans,
for soldiers on both sides
wanting home,
no singling out
from aching god,

adopted babies
from Korea
never allowed
to join this sisterhood.

I tucked his tune inside
my breath of reed
and went another way.

Out from the Wash

*Besides maybe the suit, is any single item of men's clothing
more freighted with potential meaning than the hoodie?*
  – "The Cultural History of the Hoodie"

I see you. As you never see yourself.
Walking out in one of your three white hoodies.

You choose the style and the color.
To burl up your hands in kangaroo pockets.

Cover your bald scalp from the chill.
White to be safe, visible in darkness

as if cars coming home
never respect sidewalks.

And you will be safe.
You are not a man of color.

You are not a teenager. You don't defy
or threaten anyone. Monk-like,

an innocent in histories of hooded men.
Some of whom attracted

or wreaked the deadliest mayhem.
That's beside the point to you,

the dribbler, splasher man
who drinks coffee lying down.

Your spill-palette of mustard and yard dirt
makes you the neighborhood's dirty old man

in dog-walk hoodies I bleach to perfect whiteness.
The word I heard young meant clean.

Mardi Gras Beads

A dazzle of gold and red plastic strands puddle
inside a seldom-opened drawer.

That October after Katrina, I lived behind chain link
in a FEMA compound – guardsmen with rifles
at the Algiers water treatment plant.
I slept inside a fleshy flapping tent,
like inside a wet lung.

Beyond the fence a golden retriever,
a basset hound and a beagle begged
for some share of our 5,000-calorie lunches
that FEMA packed.

The black woman who did not evacuate
her splintered house told me,
her fingers and mine clutched into fence wire
from opposite sides,
"This was God's judgment on our wickedness."

Trumpets and sax played Katrina's second line
over dregs of last year's hurled beads.

I do not see wicked,
just cheap sparkle snarled
in a naked tree.

Portland's Waterfront History

If my hometown is a *Portlandia* joke, it's a shaggy dog story
about a burly German Shepherd chasing Canada geese
up the waterfront. Muddy pawprints. A couples' brisk-walk chat
about gluten-free sambusas near the police memorial.

If it's an epic, then it's the lineage of birthright river people,
ten thousand gathered on these banks where geese feed now,
their fires burning below drum-talk of fish, trade and mates.
This park named for Elizabeth Caruthers, first white settler.

If a discarded history book, yellow at the edges, then it's not
the down-played flood allowed to destroy red-lined Vanport,
but more often sepia photos of two rich white men
who flipped a coin to name a bustling stumptown.

Today on the northernmost stone bench, I read Stafford.
Star-clusters of cherry blossoms sway overhead, blessing
thirteen granite slabs carved with Nikkei poems. And names
of internment camps. His voice: *Now is made out of ghosts.*

The Night I Didn't Stand Up

That rock concert in New Haven took me by surprise
and why – the national anthem and the crowd was ready.
As one, the many stood and hooted for the band.

I didn't, a white girl whose knees knocked.
Angry under the videos of carpet bombing
of Cambodia, over-the-top, over-the edge saturation
killing in Cambodia. This was my country tis of thee.

I sat in protest. Forty years later a quarterback kneeled
with more courage than I had in that pot-smoke crowd.
I ducked when some guy yelled I should stand.
There are times when you can't, when the wrong

is too great, and the great isn't great enough. So when
Judge Ruth says it's wrong not to stand but not illegal,
I know it can be right and the only thing you can do.
Better to let wrong drive you to your knees

than sit like a numb ass.

The White Peacock
(Pavo cristatus mut. alba)

*What we use to determine race is really nothing more than
some haphazard physical characteristics, cultural histories,
and social conventions that distinguish one group from another.*
— Kareem Abdul-Jabbar

This not-so-rare bird sleeps, eats, mates
and twerks like colorful others. Does it think
it deserves more, is loftier, has privilege?
This is not albinism, just a genetic wrinkle
that drained pigment from plumage.

The whites come out as a hue of gardenias
or the rose ineptly named *innocence*.
Peacocks of the manse wink india-blue eyes,
cold-seeing awareness and java-green
farewell feathers shimmying away.

White Girls

Cede to other women skin
tints of caramel, taffy, and fancy maple,
heady Jamaican vanilla extract
in amber glass. The glow
of copper wire. Oxides,
raw or burnt sienna.
The roughed-up walnut heartwood
deepened on roofs
of the Lower Ninth Ward.
The songs black poets sing.

Eyeball my elbows.
Cabbage whitenesses,
garden spawn. Folded water
in a rapids' raceway.
Stretch-skin of tambourines.
The background of poker cards
common as toothpicks,
rolled paper on the Marlboro,
whipped froth of separated eggs.
Salt. Milky soap. Cores
of candy apples and bananas.
We are wedding dress
and baby's breath. Pale
like airborne chalk and moist smoke.

We are leather-bound family bibles
and derivative dictionaries
of pearl linen cover cloth.
Our ivory endnotes press
shut glossaries of what little we know.

Body Language

The crows at my mailbox fear how I wave my hallelujah hands then hop back for their second chance at the cat kibble I lay down for them. Honeybees arriving at my garden for morning's feast seem to know – or trust – I won't hurt them as I yank away dry blooms of blue geraniums. They could brandish stinger retribution, but sharing the gold of morning, they read me right. At the theater, some people won't sit next to me. I cannot sit still. I jiggle my feet, kick my legs. Particularly in the second act, when the married couple confronts how they don't always like their kids and their kids seem to not like them at all. Antsy. I fidget like a flock of startled grackles, ants on moving day. What I can't figure is how that kid sat through Bible study at Emanuel AME Church and never gave away the gun-burden in his heart.

Ebony and Ivory

for Margaret Patrick and Ruth Eisenberg

Margaret learned to play piano at 8, practicing on a paper keyboard.
She went to a conservatory, accompanied a church choir and The Duke.

Ruth played the piano at first to please her husband who promised
to do the housework if she would learn using his methods.

In 1982, each suffered a stroke in New Jersey.
Ruth was 80, Margaret 69.

Margaret lost much of her speech, could not move her right side,
and wished she were dead.

Ruth regained some mobility with a walker but could not use her left side,
she who had toured with her husband, offering clinics on piano playing.

They met at a post-stroke therapy group at a New Jersey senior center.
Program Director Millie McHugh introduced them.

Margaret, meet Ruth who plays with her left hand.
Ruth, meet Margaret who plays with her right.

The two women, one black, one white, talked of Chopin,
his Waltz in D-flat major, Op. 64, No. 1.

The Minute Waltz. 138 measures to be played in one minute
when the pianist is able. They sat side by side on the bench.

First came gigs at senior center parties. Then hospitals.
A reporter named them Ebony and Ivory.

The New York Times. CNN. A call from Oprah.
Chats with Brokaw. An appearance with Liberace.

Ebony and Ivory – widowed grandmothers
bowed to applause in the pews,

shared a minute's work neither could do alone,
one bench and two hands, side by side.

Nomenclature

Between 1919 and 1959, humblebees became known as bumblebees. Some say the cause was the advancement of aeronautics. Smooth airplane takeoffs made the bee seem lurchy and unfocused. The old word *humblebees* paid homage to repetitive work, the respect every gardener owes an unassuming pollinator, but usages evolve. I'm at peace with bumblebees – and hope to live to see the Edmund Pettus Bridge with a new name.

Let's Hear It for the Horses

One million dead in the Civil War,
if you count the mules.
Which I do.

I say, blowtorch the rebel men
off their statue mounts and keep
the horses prancing on their pedestals.

They were not traitors
to their country, showed no sign
of caring who they carried,

black or white, male or
female. No one questions
their service to equality.

They did the work
they were asked to do
without a nod at glory.

Out of My Dream of a Man in a White Sheet Carrying a Sign: THIS IS WRATH

Little by little we shall make circles of these triangular stars
— Sonia Sanchez

Two farm dogs bedded in the kitchen wake me
from a night terror. I tiptoe toward the barking dogs
in my white nightgown through the darkness.
A touch to the stove, a knife on the breadboard,
a child's chair on my way to the back door.
Flip the latch. The dogs race away in outrage
into an October Milky Way.

Last week a raccoon ripped off the head
of a white hen. At dawn, her neck hole
swarmed with yellow jackets.

Deer sneak in for apples and pears.
Coyotes sing in the hills.
The ground squirrels grab at duck eggs.
At sunset a bald eagle flew
over the meat chickens' hutch.

These dogs patrol fences. Their job is to clamor
up fear. I follow their progress
from the back door. Jagged yawps near the orchard.
The wine-grape enclosure. Henhouse.
Lucia, the Cinta pig, near the barn.
The field plowed for pasture grass.

Spent, the dogs lope back,
sniffing wind-swept midnight.
My toes on the transom are cold.
My fingers comb the dogs' heads,
ask where faith finds gentle swaddling.

Portland's ICE Center As the Crow Flies

Less than two miles from the horse-race track
where the Japanese reported first for detention.

Less than two miles from my home,
rain tapping on umbrellas, clutches

of old men and women from churches,
we watch the line of golden people

wait in the chill to be called in for processing
in a huge glass and steel building too crowded

to hold them all. More women
than men, babes in arms with blankets

over their heads, strollers and toddlers.
Documents tucked deep in folders.

Dark-windowed ICE vans pull through the metal
fence, disappear. Twenty-foot gates clang down.

By the front doors, agents with guns and pepper spray
monitor metal detectors, guide the people to remove shoes,

sit on a bench, get swallowed up with the busywork
of residency, translation, apprehension.

After an hour, a small woman with a brave smile exits.
She can stay for six months. We witnesses applaud.

A man here for twenty years has never been called in
before to be processed, to be pinpointed

as to where he is and what he is doing working
for the County. He's more talkative than a little girl

with braids who burrows into her mother's skirt.
This cold queue waits for processing, a cannery word

that once meant Oregon berries, salmon, and green beans.
Now it means people. Processed people. Who live here

not far from all their people who matter.

Simple Signs & Messages

What does not kill us makes us stronger. – Friedrich Nietzsche

Someone spray-painted that graffiti on plywood
in New Orleans after Katrina –
a busty woman in a blue dress points to a future
of muddy plywood sodden in oily water.
Some artist believed Nietzsche

like I believe in postcards, hundreds I've sent.

At our thrift store donated postcards are eighteen cents each.
Florida flamingos, Outer Banks beaches, a bald eagle,
the Museum of African American History and Culture,
a humpback breaching in the Tongass, moon over Hokkaido
– and 95 others

for legislators.
Shine light on healthcare (Presque Isle Light).
Keep public lands forested (Mt. Hood from Lolo Pass).
Support diversity and refugees (Amish buggy at sunset).
Protect health care (Tennessee State Veteran Home).
Save Planned Parenthood (Portrait of Sojourner Truth).
Make us stronger in love (Fanny Brawne's house in Hampstead).

Make us stronger in love.

The Star Guard

I didn't sign up to guard American flags or burn bras.
When the Buddhist monk set himself on fire,
I wanted an extinguisher.

This morning found me whacking roses,
vicious with loppers. My car in for a tune-up.
Small repairs.

Big work - guarding air, water, birds,
rights of shaking people in detention,
fearing the Civil War come round again.

A red, white and blue sign out front
has words where a flag's stars go –
In Our America.

Phrases in the stripes
promise attending
to lives with needs.

Stars to guard.

Who Am I to Say?

Tell my story, begs the past, as if it was a prayer for an imagined life or a life that's better than the life you live.
— Terrance Hayes

Who am I to tell this story?
A white woman pushing seventy,

remembering words I wish I had not said,
door locks hammered down

against young black men on rain-slick city streets.
I am not at risk. Not a victim.

At my 50th high school reunion a man said
I had been quiet and smart back then.

Is that who I was? Am? A weak trickle
in drought never asking why so quiet?

When the Oregon AG's office investigated
everyone who had ever tweeted

#blacklivesmatter, did they laugh at me?
Dickinson sat out the Civil War,

called it an oblique place
as she peeked through lace drapes.

On these streets now I seek to do
the work Whitman urges me to do.

Three Blind Women March on Washington

Hesiod named three blind daughters of the sea –
Dread, Horror, and Alarm – witnesses who hint
of precipitous falls, unseen turns to worse.

Sharing one eye, those daughters' murky sense
of why sailed before them. My threesome in Washington
follow where Helen Keller moved with 8,000 suffragettes

in 1913 to protest Woodrow Wilson's inauguration,
blacks behind whites. Now these three, arms linked,
white-caned, eyes white to the march of women and men,
caught in a throng of slow steps, a swirl of signs

they cannot read. Beside me.
I ask, *Do you need help?*
You know where you're going?

They nod their intentions
and direction. We join the throng
of march past monuments to old men,

Reverend King, museums for history
of Native and African Americans,
repaved streets we take to again.

Why My Pussy Hat Is Purple with a Stretched Thread of Silver Silk

You know those little girls with the pink skirts,
with pink sneakers that light up when the heel strikes?
See how they grab a pink hairbow or ruffled socks
of faded lavender at a certain age?

I was never one of those. Whatever pink I bloomed
darkened over decades to a rusty purple,
like dried blood, a certain pride in the scars
that turned me out to march over and over again

beside pink and variegated pussies with signs,
peace symbols, Black Lives Matter banners.
When I put on my pointy ears, see how perfect
aging mauve seems, one tarnished thread through it.

Despite what women learned of hard,
I held on to luster through my times.

Compassion

Common advice – walk in his shoes.
Feel rubs where her socks wrinkle,
soles worn holey to rough heel scuffs,
ankles caved into weariness.

Then look through her eyes, sink
into her negatives. Glance
to bare feet and to the sides
where slippery things glide.
Where a brain finds fear.

Feel her mind suspect
how much is unfair, unstated,
undreamed, out of reach.
So far away from your start,
your day, your peachiness.

NOTES

Page 6: "Deerfield, Illinois 1959." Information regarding the City of Deerfield, Illinois in 1959 is taken from *But Not Next Door*, by Harry and Davis Rosen (Ivan Oblensky Inc., 1962).

Page 18: "Letters from Union Soldiers" refers to over 60 letters from Civil War battlefields sent by Sergeant-Major William Lewis and Voluntary Indiana Infantry Privates Benjamin Dunn, Joseph C. Dunn, P. C. Dunn and John Dunn to my Great-Grandmother Annie Dunn.

Page 24: "Advanced Placement American History." This high school class was structured around reading the Inaugural Addresses of each President in turn. Two addresses especially relevant to *How I Learned to Be White*:

I have no purpose, directly or indirectly, to interfere with the institution of slavery in the States where it exists. I believe I have no lawful right to do so, and I have no inclination to do so. – Abraham Lincoln, First Inaugural Address, March 4, 1861

We, the people, declare today that the most evident of truths—that all of us are created equal—is the star that guides us still; just as it guided our forebears through Seneca Falls, and Selma, and Stonewall; just as it guided all those men and women, sung and unsung, who left footprints along this great Mall, to hear a preacher say that we cannot walk alone; to hear a King proclaim that our individual freedom is inextricably bound to the freedom of every soul on Earth. – Barack Obama, Second Inaugural Address, January 21, 2013

Page 37: "Out from the Wash." "The Cultural History of the Hoodie" was posted on the *Put This On* website, September 20, 2015.

Page 48: "My Dream of a Man in White Sheet Carrying a Sign: THIS IS WRATH." The line from Sonia Sanchez is from "Aaayee Babo" (Praise God) in *Shake Loose My Skin*.

Page 53: "Who Am I to Say?" What Walt Whitman urges Americans to do is evident in his lines appearing on page x in the front matter.

ABOUT THE AUTHOR

Tricia Knoll grew up in Highland Park, Illinois on Chicago's north shore. She holds degrees in literature from Stanford University (BA) and Yale University (MAT). Her poetry has appeared widely in many journals including *Barrow Street Review; Columbia Journal Online; Verse Virtual; Written River;* and more. Six of her poems have been nominated for Pushcart Prizes.

She has spent several years investigating how privilege and race affect her life, work that began after serving on Portland's Human Rights Commission with special concerns for street people and people with disabilities. She herself suffers from a speech disability.

Knoll lives in Portland, Oregon with two dogs and a kind husband. She tends a landscape of Pacific Northwest native plants with gardens devoted to pollinators, roses and organic vegetables.

Please visit her website, triciaknoll.com.

This book is set in the Adobe Garamond typeface, which had its genesis in 1988 when type-designer Robert Slimbach visited the Plantin-Moretus Museum in Antwerp, Belgium, to study its collection of Claude Garamond's metal punches and typefaces. During the mid-fifteen hundreds, Garamond—a Parisian punch-cutter—produced a refined array of book types that combined an unprecedented degree of balance and elegance, for centuries standing as the pinnacle of beauty and practicality in type-founding. Slimbach has created an entirely new interpretation based on Garamond's designs and on compatible italics cut by Robert Granjon, Garamond's contemporary.

To order additional copies of this book
or other Antrim House titles, contact the publisher at

Antrim House
21 Goodrich Rd., Simsbury, CT 06070
860.217.0023, AntrimHouse@comcast.net
or the house website (www.AntrimHouseBooks.com).

•

On the house website
in addition to information on books
you will find sample poems, upcoming events,
and a "seminar room" featuring supplemental biography,
notes, images, poems, reviews, and
writing suggestions.

www.ingramcontent.com/pod-product-compliance
Lightning Source LLC
Chambersburg PA
CBHW021158080526
44588CB00008B/403